A
CAR STOPS
AND A
DOOR OPENS

A Car Stops And A Door Opens

Christopher Bursk

CavanKerry ❖ Press LTD.

CavanKerry Press Ltd.
Fort Lee, New Jersey
www.cavankerrypress.org

Publisher's Cataloging-in-Publication
(Provided by Quality Books, Inc.)
    Bursk, Christopher, author.
        [Poems. Selections]
        A car stops and a door opens / Christopher Bursk. —
    First edition.
        pages cm — (Notable voices series)
        ISBN 978-1-933880-60-0
        1. Dysfunctional families—Poetry. 2. Psychic trauma
    in children—Poetry. 3. Prisoners—Poetry. 4. Sex
    offenders—Poetry. 5. Poetry. I. Title. II. Series:
    Notable voices.
    PS3552.U765A6 2017   811'.54
                    QBI16-900090

Cover art courtesy of Bernadette Karpa
Cover and interior text design by Ryan Scheife, Mayfly Design
First Edition 2017, Printed in the United States of America

Cavankerry Press is proud to publish the works of established poets of merit and distinction.

Cavankerry Press is grateful for the support it receives from the New Jersey State Council on the Arts.

ALSO BY CHRISTOPHER BURSK

Standing Watch (1978)
Little Harbor (1982)
Place of Residence (1983)
Making Wings (1983)
Places of Comfort, Places of Justice (1987)
The Way Water Rubs Stone (1988)
The One True Religion (1997)
Cell Count (1998)
Working the Stacks (2002)
Ovid at Fifteen (2003)
The Improbable Swervings of Atoms (2005)
The First Inhabitants of Arcadia (2006)
The Infatuations and Infidelities of Pronouns (2011)
The Boy with One Wing (2013)
Selected Poems (2014)
Unthrifty Loveliness (2015)

For Pam and Herb Perkins-Frederick

&

for Lorraine Henrie Lins, Christine McKee,
Deda Kavanagh, Camille Norvaisas,
and Katherine Falk, Marilee May Morris,
Pat Goodrich, and all the community of poets
who nourished Pam's and Herb's souls

&

for Mary Ann
who nourishes my soul

And little bird,
what have you given up
for this gift of yours?

How many dreams slid
from palm to palm—
how many more must?

So many bills
yet to be paid.

BERNADETTE KARPA

I saw a wasp bury his head in black pillows,
then rise to clean his antennae through gentle jaws,
and as I watched and withheld my hand,
I imagined it was my own head submerged
in sweet juice, but still able to
breathe, still able to cleanse myself at will,
still able to submerge myself, again.

HERB PERKINS-FREDERICK

Circuitous routes in the vale of soul-making
are not meant to be undone, to become straight highways.

DR. HELEN WILSON

CONTENTS

III.

IV.

A
CAR STOPS
AND A
DOOR OPENS

A Car Stops and a Door Opens

The first time I hadn't expected
a thing so momentous
would take so little time.
When I got out of the car, I was surprised
to find street lamps looked the same,
though they didn't seem interested
in shedding light. It was all I could do
not to stop strangers
and tell them everything, as one might
after being abducted by aliens
and subject to experiments.
At home, I thought even the cat would guess
I was not the same boy
who'd fed her just before leaving.
I was tempted to brag to my brother.
Finally, here was something I'd done
he hadn't. The second time it happened
I realized how lucky I was
to have survived the first. I watched
the car drive off and stood in a downpour
and let myself be hit again
and again by the obliging rain.
There was no third time. The car stopped
and I didn't get in.

I.

Without Desire, the Bird Would Not Fly

So take its wings
and all that compels it
towards the sky.

ELIZABETH AUSTIN

The Expulsion from Paradise
Masaccio—1427

It can't be comfortable walking around
with vegetation rubbing against your pubis.
Were Adam and Eve trying to wear the Garden
out of its gates? Imagine being kicked out of Paradise
and not permitted to bring anything of your own,
except a few weeds to remind you of Eden's fragrance.

One suitcase! That's all you're allowed,
mother had said as she dragged my brother downstairs
and outside. Our father came home
to find him asleep on the front steps.
Maybe it's not surprising we kept dancing
long after our mother pushed open our door—
offering up every part of ourselves to air and light,
flaunting our hips, wagging our testicles
as if they'd been created for this very purpose.

Surely she was just having one of her bad days;
surely she'd see how reasonable it was
for us to want to hop up and down, unencumbered
by anything as silly as underpants.
When the ambulance arrived, I watched from the bushes,
as I imagined Eden's animals must have,
not knowing what was happening but sensing
it would change their lives forever.

She'll be back in a few days, our father kept saying,
months later. I didn't have to be a genius
to figure out that it was my and my brother's fault
our mother had been expelled from Paradise.

At least Masaccio's Eve gives in to her pain, wailing
at the world as if it might relent.
Adam cowers, hands before his eyes
as if they're to blame for all this trouble,
and he's not going to trust them with anything
now, not even his own nakedness,
much less Eve's. For the first time
but not the last, shame is trying to change
what cannot be changed.

Years later, when I look at this picture,
Adam's and Eve's feet seem as exposed
as their newly highlighted genitals

and just as much at the world's mercy,
their soles finding out how unforgiving
the path would prove. After a lifetime
of meandering Eden's meadows,
they'd had no time to harden to the journey ahead.

The Mouth Knows Grief

After the boy's cat "died,"
his mother gave him the ashes,
thinking maybe that'd stop him from asking again
just where Bouncy was.
Bouncy's in the box on your bureau.
His mother didn't have to say that.
All she needed to do was to point.

One day when no one else was home
the boy opened the box
expecting a little of Bouncy's softness to sift
through his fingers, but he found instead
of paws and whiskers
grit so fine he could hold it in a spoon.

It had to be the perfect spoon,
one with filigree on its handle,
and then he dipped it in what was left
of his cat and held to his lips
what could have passed for an exotic sugar.
Oooh, you say. *Disgusting,* you say.
Didn't he choke? you ask.

But what if you're in elementary school
and the only creature you ever trusted
not to hurt you
proves to be in a box with a gold latch
and you're hungry,
you've never been so hungry in your life?

Come with me, he says

If the light decides to take human form
and give itself a name from medieval romance,
who am I to question its intentions?
I do what it wishes
and apparently this evening it wishes to become Alwyn
with hazel eyes and half a smile
that whispers, *Yes, I know what it's like*
to suffer, but I also know
what it's like to find a path through the darkest of trees.

My father often forgets which son I am.
My mother cannot be trusted with a knife.
My brothers tire of explaining me to friends,
and the kids at school grow bored with beating me up.
So when a boy appears at the window
and takes my hand and holds it to his lips
and says, *Here's your one chance.*
Come with me. You won't regret it,

I pack only what I need: my Ted Lepcio baseball card,
my army of spent matches,
the key I found in second grade and now go nowhere without,
a passage from Leviticus I ripped out of the Bible.
A boy that looks like disheveled light
that's just thrown on its clothes
but wouldn't mind taking them off again
opens the window
and leads me onto the roof.

I am prepared to leave this world.
I've been ready all my life.

Prisoner of War, Death by Poison, Cat Burglar

What do you and your imaginary friend Alwyn do?
your brother asks when you finally admit
why you pushed a chair against the door
and wouldn't let him in.
Timothy is used to being in charge
of the games you play: *Murder the Prince,*
Walk Though Fire, Come Back
from the Dead. You're always the one lashed
to a tree, the one with singed heels,
the one whose throat is slit,
but occasionally you want to die
in someone's arms
besides your brother's, someone your own age
and who better than Alwyn?
He may be imaginary but he's tough
enough to make you sit still
while he administers warm washcloths
to the places you've rubbed raw,
the marks on your legs
where the matches gave up
hope of burning your entire body.
Alwyn doesn't ask anything more of you
than that you fall asleep
next to him. *What have you been doing?*
Timothy demands
when he climbs through the window
you forgot to lock shut.
You're naked, hair mussed up,
a little blood at the corner of your lips.
That's just how your brother likes you.

Leviticus 16:20–22

Because he can't afford a goat,
my brother has decided I'll do.
So I get down on all fours,
and Timothy places his palm on my head.
What good fortune!
Today I'm not going to be slaughtered!
Instead I receive the good weight
of my brother's hand on me,
proud to be a resting place
for the very same fingers
that turn serpent into staff
and then persuade it to bear almonds.
At bedtime when Timothy reminds me
of the Israelites' transgressions,
he adds our own: every afternoon
we've danced from bed to bed;
every china cup we've shattered;
all the damage we blamed on the dog
keeping silent while he howled outside;
every lie we told on our mother;
every night we wished our father dead,
then brought him back to life
without his knowing;
every visit we refused to kiss Grandma,
who wouldn't let go of us till we did.
Timothy marks me for God
by making small incisions behind my ears
and in my knees' hollows.
I am to carry our sins
into a solitary, dark, inaccessible land.
The Bible doesn't say what happens to the goat
in the wilderness, but I know.

Am I not to drink the cup that the father has given me?

No one else was willing to be Judas, so I agreed
in return for a few good lines and the chance
to bestow a kiss of betrayal on Clarkie Truesdale

towards whom, on opening night, I moved
with the authority of rain
brushing aside Apostle Paul and knocking over Apostle Peter.

On my tiptoes I surprised the unsuspecting lips
of eighth grade's tallest boy
who—clearly tempted to wipe away my spittle—

stayed in character. At rehearsal after rehearsal
I'd merely grazed his hairline
as my Sunday school teacher had coached.

So why in front of parents and schoolmates
did I elect to turn pariah and plant my mouth
so explicitly on his? I can still taste those lips

my lips pumped for information:
chapped but softer than expected.
It hadn't seemed right to kiss the Son of God

on the brow, as a grandfather might,
or on the cheek, the way an aunt might.
From His mouth had come the Great Commandment

and though ours was a Unitarian church attended
by Ralph Waldo Emerson's befuddled descendants,
all Lent we'd led up to this man's sacrifice

of his human body for our divine souls.
The least I could do was offer Him a little tongue.

Madonna with Child and Eight Angels
Sandro Botticelli—1478

Eight long-legged kids with pageboy haircuts, each
    holding an extravagant bloom over his head
    the way he might an umbrella.

Eight high school freshmen performing a cappella for Mary
    who's just given up a promising career and looks now
    as if nothing will cheer her.

Eight lads serenading the Virgin
    and her child, who long before the camera's invention
    seems to be posing for it
    as if he already knows his destiny
    and wants every stage of it recorded.

Eight potential babysitters for the Son of God
    who worry that any minute he might start bawling
    for his mother's nipple,
    at which point where will it be safe for the boys to look?

Eight neighborhood pals just before their voices change
    singing doo-wop,
    as if they intend to hit all the high notes while they can.

Eight teenagers jockeying for position around Mary,
    each with a crush on her.

Eight youths, four on either side of Mary
    as if they were her wings, and, should she wish,
    they'd transport her anywhere she desired.

Eight gangly ninth-graders holding white lilies and singing
　　from gem-encrusted hymnals and still
　　it's not sufficient to bring a smile to the face
　　of Mary who knows there's not enough music in the world
　　to make up for all the agony to come.

Morte d'Arthur

1

Don't fidget, Timothy reproaches me
as he cuts the tin
left from one of our mother's old art projects
and molds it to my hips. If you hope
to rescue anyone, you need the right equipment:
faulds, greaves, brassards, pauldrons.
It requires all the patience my brother has
to teach me to walk
coated in metal, much less to wield a halberd.
Even out of armor—ah blessed
nakedness—I move as if I still have it on,
and my body has forgotten how to bend at elbow
and knee. *Does a knight watch television?*
my brother reminds me. *Does he take an afternoon off*
just because of a cut lip?
We're going to keep thrusting and parrying.
smiting and being smitten till we're ready.
We are never ready.

2

Most boys would prefer to be knight
than squire, but most boys don't have a brother
like Timothy whom even the sun recognizes
as a chevalier worthy of devotion.
The light goes out of its way
to make a path for him in the woods
or wait for him as he bathes in the river,
so it seems fitting I too offer myself
in his service. If the sun isn't too proud
to polish his armor, the least I can do

is assist with soap and water.
I bear Timothy's gleaming shield into battle
and do not forsake his side
all day but step in front of arrows
aimed for his heart, take the blows
meant for my liege lord
and fall, still waving his banner
and gasping his name. Over and over I expire
with my brother's kiss on my brow.
What more can I ask? How often
does a boy get to make the supreme sacrifice?
I die almost every Saturday. And some Sundays too.

3

You'd think sacking a city would be simple
but we know from experience it isn't.
You try disemboweling a Turk or cutting out a Saracen's heart.
Of course Mordred turns on Arthur.
Of course Guinevere's eyes wander.
How could a woman remain faithful to a man
as preoccupied as Arthur was
tracking down dragons and dragging England
out of the Dark Age? He turned out to be even busier
than our father. On his rare days home
we insist our father read *Morte d'Arthur*,
all the way to the end. We love how his voice falls
when he speaks Arthur's last words.
It's always a surprise to learn our father can feel
as deeply as we do. *Read it again,*
we beg him as all three of us crouch
over the King languishing in good Sir Bedivere's embrace.
We want this death to last forever.

4

Lie down here.
Timothy points to a place on the floor
the moon has already chosen,
and then he lies next to me
and rests his head on my lap,
as if the only palliative to make his wounds tolerable
would be to strip off my armor
and make me suffer too
just a little. *It won't hurt*
that much, he promises. I'd do anything
to make my brother's pain less
so I don't cry out.
There's no one in the house to hear me
except my brother. *Shhh,*
he says. *It'll be all right.*
I'm sorry, he says. *It's okay,* I say
and press my head deep into the pillow
that does everything it can
to stop the hurt.

5

Tonight, you be the Lady of the Lake
one last time. My brother holds out a dress
from our mother's closet, the dark velvet
she wore the week before she vanished.
I lift my arms and my brother makes sure the softness
falls over my shoulders. He's dressing me
in night sky—the lamps off everywhere in the house
so even he can't see me
at first. *Pretend you are rising from the lake.*
Here, hold the sword up high.
It has glow-in-the-dark stars fastened to its hilt.
I am offering him the only light
left in the universe. He takes it from my hand.

The Benefits of Burning Oneself

See how promiscuously the skin gives in
to the flame? It reveals no shred

of dignity, attached as it is to this needy
and compromised body.

That's the beauty of matches.
Fire requires only a few seconds

to do what's asked of it.
It wastes no time on self-pity.

In the interval it takes you to light a match
and introduce it

to your arm, you're not worrying
about anything you said

or shouldn't have, did and shouldn't have.
No, you're focused

on one clear fact: your right to feel pain.
It's not often you get a chance

to be victim and perpetrator and witness
at the same time. To your shame

no matter how obligingly flesh agrees
to shrivel,

you can't seem to hold still
under the flames' interrogation.

Luckily fire doesn't care if you've flinched
before. Pain's generous that way: willing

to let those it chooses
prove themselves over and over.

It lets you try again
to learn what you can't bear and what you can.

Indigo White, Blanc de Fard, Alabaster!

Paint me! I nagged my brother
I wanted to be pearl and burnt almond,
parchment and ivory,
as if one tube of paint couldn't do justice
to even an ordinary kid like me, a whole palette
required to capture the complexities of my face.
Paint me? I asked when he took out his brushes
on the rare occasions he decided it was okay,
at seventeen, to do something not aimed
at getting into college or getting laid.
Paint me! Meaning *make me the center of your world,*
at least for today. I'd have perched on a rock
or sprawled on the grass, as naked
as my brother wished me to be, stayed still
as long as he needed. Finally
he'd have to acknowledge I existed
again, devote at least a morning
and maybe an afternoon to adjusting my shoulders
and tilting my head. And then there'd be two
of me—one on the canvas and one
posing by the window—and my brother
would keep glancing back and forth
between us. I'd be free
to stare at him. That's one of the privileges
of posing. *Paint me,*
I begged, as if at fourteen,
I still had the right to request what I longed for,
my brother's hands remembering me
even after he took them away;
I'd be the smudge of magenta under his nails,
a little zinc oxide on his forehead
he'd keep missing in the shower.
He'd not be able to wash me off for weeks.

Dr. Levin

Where I lived, if boys thought what I thought
they were sent to doctors.

And so I told Dr. Levin everything
but the truth. You try to be honest when you're sixteen

and supine on a couch. Of course I failed
to mention the boy whose math notes I borrowed

so my hand had an excuse to brush against his.
I wasn't worried about being queer

as much as being pathetic.
Everything in the doctor's office told me

to keep my thoughts to myself—even his photographs
careful not to reveal too much,

the smiling kids on his desk as manufactured
as those found in picture frames in stores.

I'd never seen so many books
I'd no interest in reading. An erudite

but kind man, Dr. Levin said very little
about himself—certainly nothing of what I discovered

years after he terminated our visits:
that he'd lost two sisters in a nightclub fire

and a brother in the war in Tunisia.
Listen! I wanted to command the doctor

and hold his hand to my heart.
I was just a sophomore and still trusted in the heart.

I Have Been Faithful to Thee, Cynara, in My Fashion

What do you do if you're a junior in high school
and the girl you expected to see every day
for the rest of your life
finally listens to her parents and agrees
to move with them across the ocean
to a country so foreign you don't even know its capital

and when you tell her you'll write every morning
and every evening, she presses her hand
to your lips and tells you, *No.*
No letters, no phone calls.
She's crying too but not the tears
of someone who's going to change her mind.
No. That's the last thing she says

when you show up on moving day
with roses. Did you think she'd carry them all the way
to Estonia? *No,*
she says as you follow her to the car door
and try to look so sad
there's no way she can forget you.

Her little brother's sobbing
as if he's the one, all along, who loved you
the most. But Cynthia?
Though it takes a while for her to free her hand
from yours—you're a knot
she must tug at to untangle—
she's already gone before she gets in the car.

No. You pretend it's a kiss
she's blowing you.

You catch it on your fingertips and hold it there
as if it meant something completely different.
You're seventeen
and used to lying to yourself.

What He Doesn't Tell the Frat Brothers Interviewing Him

That he just discovered he was born with a single wing.
That when he looks in the mirror he can't see it

but knows it's there.
That when he and his girlfriend make love, he leaves his shirt on.

That one side of him is heavier than the other.
That it makes him limp a little as he walks.

That the wing must have been there all his life
but he didn't notice it.

That he thinks of it constantly now:
how it must be impossibly ugly,

how it might be improbably beautiful,
how sometimes you can't tell the difference.

That he will not let any doctor examine him.
That it's a growth

any doctor would want to cut out of him.
That he hates it.

That he would never part with it.
That it is his only mark of distinction.

What Doesn't Get Said in Therapy

You claim to be a monster?
                    What presumption!
          Come back
when you've strangled a child
                    or sodomized your sister
          or poisoned a city's water supply
or set off a bomb in a crowd of people
                    who won't get a chance
          as you have now
to go into therapy and complain
                    their father is a satyr
          or their mother's Medusa.
You don't have it in you
                    to be ogre or Cyclops,
          the doctor scolds
and hands you a prescription.
                    I've seen real monsters,
          he says, looking out the window
as he often does, finding
                    what's blowing in the trees
          far more interesting than anything
you might say. *Don't embarrass yourself,*
                    he scolds. *No monster*
          claims to be a monster.
You get to be one the old-fashioned way,
                    the hard way.
          You earn it.

Lorca in Roxbury

¡Qué esfuerzo!
¡Qué esfuerzo del caballo por ser perro!

Though I don't know much Spanish
that doesn't stop me from reading Lorca
on the floor to twelve-year-old Felix.
It doesn't bother Felix
that Lorca's horse is trying to be a dog
and Lorca's dog trying to be a swallow
and the swallow, a bee
as long as Felix can do what he likes most: make sails
billow and flap on ships so huge
the winds are propelling small cities
across the sea, decks filled with furnaces and forges,
anvils and assembly lines, whole factories of workers.
Though Felix's ocean looks determined
not to let anyone cross it
without a struggle, his crew doesn't seem worried
about being swept towards the earth's edge.
Felix never answers why he's drawing
what he does, though he does agree
to read Lorca aloud to me in the original:
Aquella noche el rey de Harlem con una durisma cuchara
arrancaba los ojos a los cocodrilos.
He doesn't question the king of Harlem
spooning out the crocodile's eyes
anymore than that we're reading about it
in a vault in a bank in Roxbury, Massachusetts
turned into an after-school center
where now he launches a fully-rigged metropolis
teeming with carpenters and glaziers

and butchers and florists too busy to gaze up
from their lathes, open fires, and lilies
to see where they're being carried by a wind
with its work cut out too. Every night
I go home and dream of García Lorca
lying feverish in my arms, and no matter how hard I try
I can't wake him from his nightmare;
no matter how often I stroke his damp hair
I can't make his suffering any less.
And Felix? What does he dream of
who's sent a city, full sail, towards the horizon?

October 23

Not mine own fears, nor the prophetic soul

Had my Dad been sleepwalking?
What led him to travel the moonlit hall
from his room to mine,
like a messenger who, upon reaching his destination,
cannot part with the news
pressed so long to his chest, it breathes
when he does; has he held it
so tight it now belongs to him alone?
Had my father divested himself of his pajamas
because he couldn't let the tidings he bore
be compromised by anything
as trivial as clothes? For years I've tried
to make sense of my father's visit.
He didn't lift a finger to me
and only opened his mouth to sigh,
but surely he'd wanted to tell me something.
I haven't found the words yet
to figure out what it was.

The Key

Here, the man says, stopping you on the street,
is the key to my heart,
and he closes your fingers
around a real key and then vanishes so quickly
you aren't sure he'd stood next to you
and when you unclench your fist,
the sun chooses that exact moment

to congratulate the key and when you tilt it
this way and then that
it turns into an ocean vessel; then a skyline;
then a mountain range;
then three kings in search of the Christ child.
It proves too large
for every lock you insert it in.

This is the key to my heart, the man had whispered,
the way spies do
just before their throats are slit.
How can such a brief encounter change a life
that, up till then,
had no intentions of being changed?
There are too many locks in the world

for a boy to try every one, yet you pass no door
without testing it.

II.

It wouldn't surprise me a bit if I were to look up
and see all the stars blown to one side of the sky.

LORRAINE HENRIE LINS

News from a foreign country came

1 *As if my treasures and my joys lay there*

Why don't you take off your shirt?
I'm learning how to be a masseur and yours
is the perfect body to practice on
—such an unexpected request to come from a man
with a chair endowed in his name.
Did my professor intend to give up Richard Crashaw
for back rubs, Sir John Suckling
for latissimus dorsi, Andrew Marvell
for rhomboideus major and minor?
Say no to the author of books so expensive
only libraries could buy them?
I was already intoxicated with after-dinner liqueurs
and *They are all gone into the world of light.*
If a few gauzy conceits knocked me off my feet,
consider what an expensive cordial might do
to my semicircular canals.
If my teacher needed my back
to experiment on, didn't I owe him that much?
Here, let me help you. He undid my buttons
as if I were a child who hadn't learned
to get undressed on his own
or a son being readied for his bath.
So much of my sex life as a young man
involved staying perfectly still.
My professor's office was small, but its dark
huge. I expected the walls to open
the way they do in planetariums
to a universe waiting to be admired.
This man who knew maybe more than anyone

about the seventeenth century
wasn't about to waste time on more
than a syllable or two. *Please,*
he begged my shoulders. *Please,*
he confided to my ribs.

2   *So let us melt and make no noise . . .*

Not till he unlaced and slipped off my shoes
and rolled down my socks,
did I realize lovemaking could commence
with the heel. Was he searching
to see if I might actually be a goddess's son
dipped in an immortal stream?
My right, then left foot arched
the way a stroked cat might.
Dr. V manipulated my soles
as he might a conceit he thoroughly enjoyed
deconstructing, toe
by toe. It might have been disarmingly creepy
if it hadn't felt so good.
Nothing in my high school Sex Ed. class
had prepared me to erupt in orgasm
from having my ankles caressed.
Afterwards, Dr. V. studied my semen
as if every thread of it merited close observation
the way one holds a spider's web to the sun
to test how far it could stretch.
Maybe I wasn't a complete disappointment.
He still had my leg muscles to knead,
my tibia and fibula to learn by heart.
I was young. Who knew what surprises
my body might have left?

3   *Behind what curtain were you so long from me hid?*

When Dr. V began paying attention to my earlobes,
finding them even more interesting
than the music of the spheres
he'd been explaining, I stopped being a kid
who slouched in the back of Brit. Lit.
trying to look as much like a juvenile delinquent
as a boy reading John Donne can.
These hands that'd written ten books
were now committed to textual analysis
of my solar plexus, a lengthy exegesis
on my inner elbow. When he kissed my neck,
my mark for the course proved the last thing
on my mind, focused, as I was, on eternity:
my eyelids and nose delineated,
my collar bone explicated,
my underarms a small digression, even my feet
expatiated on, nothing found wanting
in me, at least for that night.
How like an angel came I down.

4   *. . . my striving eye / Dazzles at it, as eternity . . .*

When I woke up, I had a blanket tucked around me
like a shipwreck survivor, not a freshman
who couldn't locate his underwear
and so put on his teacher's. I must've looked
like a kid wearing his daddy's boxers,
holding them up by the waist as I felt my way
from one dark room to another.
Professor, I kept whispering, *Professor,*
where are you? It seemed unthinkable
to address a man thrice my age

by his first name even though he'd just
invested his DNA in me.
Professor? He slept so determinedly
on the couch, I didn't have the heart
to wake him. When I think of that night—
and I think of it often—I remember the moon
lending his pudgy belly and thick arms
a sheen water might have emulated.
The afghan he'd kicked loose
I drew back over him, running my hand
though his hair as if he or I
were a prince from a faraway kingdom.

5   *Like gold to airy thinness beat*

Now that he'd tired of doing what he wanted
with my body, it was my turn
to do what I liked
with his, to watch it work
without his mind's interference;
his arms flung out, hands
fluttering as if he'd fallen asleep swimming.
I'd always wanted to look at a man
without looking away, to investigate his mouth
now under no obligation
to be clever. I even liked the penis
when it wasn't trying so hard
to be the world's best lover.
At last, I could gaze at a man as I might a tree
or pond. Leaves don't get embarrassed
by the attention paid them.
Water expects to be stared at.
Was this why I let someone my father's age
mount me—so when he fell asleep

I'd be free to play with his chest hair,
straightening each strand and letting it spring back,
finally intimate with a man
in ways I'd never dared?

6 *Hark, hard, the waters fall, fall, fall*

What I remembered most
after he rolled over and fell asleep:

not his arms holding mine down
as if I were a kid throwing a tantrum;

not his mouth nibbling my neck and shoulders,
determined to swallow my entire body,

starting with the smoothest parts of me;
not his fiddling with me,

trying a lock refusing
to accommodate its key. No, I remembered

how patiently his fingers proceeded
down my shirt,

as if showing me how to perform
the simplest of acts: undo

what once required practice to fasten:
forefinger easing down, thumb waiting below

like movers managing something unwieldy
they didn't want to drop.

I stayed as still as I could. I tried
to take in everything he was teaching me.

7 *When Thou hast done, Thou hast not done*

Afterwards, I bent over my sneakers
like a three-year-old learning to tie a knot.
Only a half an hour before, a world authority
on Dryden had found me so important
he'd left something of himself
inside me. In one night, my Ptolemaic world
turned Copernican. I'd not known
minutes could stretch the way sonnets could.

But flat on a desk with George Herbert
nudging my naked spine
and the Dean of St. Paul's for a headrest,
my professor sobbing into my neck,
and the room revolving,
I understood the music of the spheres
for the first time and swore
the moment could last a lifetime
though it proved done
almost as soon as it had begun.

8 *. . . like a great ring of pure and endless light.*

When the man ran his hands over my back
as if measuring for wings,
I knew more would be asked of my body

than it had thought itself capable,
my arms stretched
till I almost expected them to sprout feathers

and fly me, my legs content to abandon the earth.
Mounted, I hadn't been pressed down,
but exalted. With every thrust, a man had gripped me

tighter. Any moment, I might slip out of his arms
and plummet to the Earth:
Icarus in Daedalus' embrace.

Afterwards, helped to my feet
and steadied as if I'd forgotten how to walk,
I was dismissed, but didn't mind.

A seed had been planted so deep in me,
I knew it would take root.
What English major gets a chance like that:

to know what angels must know
every day of their existence:
the great ring of pure and endless light?

I had the rest of my life ahead of me
to remember.
That ought to be enough for any mortal.

III.

Think BIG! a friend says,
but I am creature of little things,
overlooked, broken.

little, I think, *little*

PATRICIA GOODRICH

The Holding Cell

Importune. Sly pulls out the word
the way a kid might a revolver
he's brought to school. He's got a whole armory
in his cell—*inarticulate, disingenuous, vacillating*—
weapons you don't have to fire
to feel their recoil, their perfect aim.
You think Shakespeare cranked out poems?
You haven't been to the Edison Detention Center
where everybody's falling in and out of love.
The sonnet proves a perfect form to master
while doing twelve to twenty-two months.
Dwayne claims he's happy to be back.
The best I could do on the streets
was squeeze in a haiku or two.
So what if he's guilty of clichés?
He's faced worse charges.
You want us to do what? Tiny asks.
I might as well have pulled a pistol
on a room full of hold-up men
and demanded they empty their pockets
of villanelles, cinquins, tankas, Pindaric odes.
I stuff ghazals in my satchel and make my getaway
snatching the number runner's sestina,
the smash-and-grab's rondeau,
and yet another ballad
where bad luck's an undercover cop,
crack cocaine a stone-cold lover.
Maybe those old recidivists—*beautiful, lonely,*
lost—might have something left
to teach us, even those snitches, the weasely
prepositions. *If we just hung out with a different crowd,*

the adverbs sigh remorsefully.
Like anyone behind bars
they know the importance of telling a tale over
and over till it's true. It doesn't matter
that they've recited the same story
before. You're looking for repeat offenders?
Open a book, turn to any page. This page.

Hulmeville Marine Dies in Car Bombing
For Cpl. Robert Parnell

Outside my window the neighbor's kid
seems to be growing muscles in the process
of jumpstarting his dad's mower. Often
cutting lawns is a suburban kid's first chance
to feel anything come alive in his hand,
spark plugs igniting, sheer urge bucking under his fingers.
He's not pushing as much as taming the mower,
that *id* with blades, all that combustion his
to do with as he wishes.
At his age, tired by the day's fourth lawn,
I'd be tempted to let the mower follow its destiny:
and cut down everything in its path
till nothing fragrant remained
standing, every rose reminded of just how irrelevant
beauty is to a blade.
This boy takes no prisoners, either,
waging battle against the infidel horde.
He has no use for belts also,
their outdated strictures,
his pants already slipping past his waist
and riding his hips. Any minute
they may slide all the way down
and he'll step out of them. The small of his back—
wars could be fought over a thing that innocent.

Bringing *The Virgin and Child* into the County Jail

What have you got there? the guard asks, not happy I'm putting him in the position of confiscating the Mother of God. Nothing in this young man's training has prepared him to decide whether or not Madonna and Christ Child ought to be contraband, though this copy of an early Renaissance painting under my arm certainly looks dangerous. Mary's bared left breast could drive anyone to a life of crime.

What are you, some sort of voyeur? Is this why you come here. So you can watch us get tents in our pants? the Ice Man bellows in a voice he uses as a weapon that'll survive even a strip search. *You don't have to be pretty to be raped,* he glares at me as if any moment he's going to burst from his chair.

Do I really think *Virgin and Child Surrounded by Angels* is going to transform a class of carjackers and shoplifters? That, on the streets again, before snatching a woman's purse, Sammy will pause to imagine how Vermeer might've painted her? Want to understand Cubism? Spend a month behind bars.

Ekphrasis. It sounds like some bad shit, says Tiny, as if I hadn't asked him to write about a painting but try a drug so new it hadn't hit the streets yet.

It takes a while before any of us looks closely at the painting. Even the Ice Man seems reluctant to be caught ogling the Virgin Mary's breasts. In the presence of this smiling, well-nourished baby, for once Nick forgets to snarl and remind everyone he's the boss of this jail. Is he too imagining a time when he'd no inkling what cross awaited him?

I Take My Granddaughter to See the Face of Jesus

You try explaining the Supper of Emmaus
to a four-year-old standing before the Son of God
in Rembrandt's 1629 oil on paper
a shadowy figure rearing back
as if about to scold not just the disciple opposite him
but the whole world. Jesus cloaked in darkness
is no comfort for Sadie
or the disciple who cowers the way a kid might
right before his kindergarten teacher punishes him.
That's not wonder on the man's face,
but terror turned craven and ugly
as terror is wont to do.
What would you do if you sat down to supper,
and a corpse seized the only other chair
and stared at you, saying nothing?
The distance between Christ and Cleopas
is that between a disappointed father
and his child. Sadie scrunches up her face
so she can see all the way to the woman
in the background, a wall of mortared night
separating her from the Christ.
Whose mother is that? Sadie asks.
Maybe the woman will bring whatever it is
she's cooking and it'll be so good
this silent, disdainful man will finally open His mouth
and even bestow a blessing,
but Sadie's not sure. Sadie doesn't like this Jesus
right now, and who can blame her?

Forensics

Before class I ask the boy who kidnapped his sister
because their mother's *a junkie* and their father *breaks things*
how he's doing, and he holds up a clear plastic bottle
with the kidney stone he passed last night,
and I try not to think about the intrepid pebble
pushing its way out of his penis.
It's difficult enough to teach
without imagining your students' private parts,
much less their pain. This evening,
my criminal justice major who spent a year in Juvie
doesn't seem quite as angry with the girls
in the back row who, two weeks ago, reported him
to the Dean. He'd trusted them
with blow-by-blow accounts of his breakup
with the evil Gina, whom he expected them to hate
as much as he did, though they'd never met her.
Now they sit as far from him
as possible, occasionally looking over and giggling.
If I were the same person I was a few years ago,
I'd smack the smile off her face.
Is he referring to his ex or the girls' ringleader
whom campus security now escorts to her car
and who, he claims, chews amphetamines for candy?
All semester he's been texting her.
I'm trying to help. But what does she do?
Where I live you don't survive if you snitch.
He often looks as if he's just been slapped
and is deciding whether to cry or hit back,
a white kid who's hung around black kids so much
he's come to suspect everyone
with blond hair and blue eyes.

For the past week, he's been making up his mind
whether to do his research essay on John Dillinger
or W. E. B. Du Bois, *Three dumb honky chicks,*
he says, *what do they know?*
The nursing student whose grandfather died last week,
the girl whose father sees her only on supervised visits,
and the Ukrainian girl who writes about anorexia
because a "friend" suffers from it.
Jesse shakes the kidney stone out of its bottle
and rolls it back and forth in his palm.

Grading Papers in the Hospital Room

Whatever spirit guides our existence,
thank you for the freshmen compositions I must grade
before tomorrow's class,
comma splices and dangling participles,
distracting my right hand
while my left begs Herb's arm
to come to a temporary truce with its restraints
and stop tugging at his catheter.
All my usually discursive friend can manage today
is *Jesus, Jesus,* as I tip his right, then his left side
while the nurse soaks free the fecal matter
that once having been inside him
seems reluctant to be parted from him now,
one of the few things still truly his,
and his fingers reach for it. I'd forgotten how exhausting
it is to let someone die, the stiff back
you get from crouching over a bed.
Nothing I say offers relief for my friend
but still I lift his palms to my lips.
Maybe his skin will carry my prayer to a part of his brain
that insists on its right to decode.
Hopefully he's too worn out
to consider the enormity of what's happening,
too preoccupied taking deep breaths
to convince his lungs to keep working.
Whatever spirit in the universe relishes
what's brilliant, thank you
for finding Herb's hospital window
so he and I can doze in the light
that doesn't care which one of us is living,
which of us is dying.

Thank you, sun, for every freckle
on Herb's legs, every distinguished hair
on his arms. For reminding me it's possible
to have shit wedged into the wrinkles
of the scrotum—and wires tangling
in flailing arms—and hands gripping so tightly
it's hard to believe they're attached to a body
that's expiring—and still be gorgeous.
Today I am going to give everyone A
despite how often they write *effect* for *affect*,
no for *know*; no, because they do they run one sentence
into another refuse to put a period
where it belongs it belongs nowhere.

What I Didn't Do Today

Though I knew the Dean was waiting for me to tell him
to go fuck himself
when he handed me the new, revised policy
on academic freedom and its limits.
I merely strangled him
in my mind, just one of many people
I could have put out of their misery today.

I didn't rip the smart phone, mid-text,
out of the pimply boy's hand and throw its urgent message
out the window. Nor did I embarrass the girl next to him
who kept drawing what looked like penises
in the margins of *Song of Myself.*

Driving home I managed not to rear-end the car
in front of me, though its driver slammed to a stop
as if he'd just seen Banquo's ghost.

Once in the front door I didn't kick the cat
who rubbed against my legs
making clear it was my fault she'd been bored all day.
Nor did I push aside my Argentine sheepdog
though his busy tongue was not what I needed
after eight hours of hyperactive kids.
I even managed not to snarl
at my wife or children, all of whom have learned by now
not to acknowledge I am home
till I'm ready to acknowledge I'm home.

When I went to vote, I didn't punch the two suits
who asked me if I was afraid of yet another four years
of socialism. Nor did I hang up

on the person who'd forgotten whom he'd called
and then remembered to ask me
to donate to the Police Benevolent Society.

I surprised my son by not berating him for his 64%
in spelling. I even gave the pizza boy a bigger tip than he expected.
Finally I let the dog jump on the bed
and the purring cat dig her nails into my thigh,
and didn't wake my wife
every time she kicked me in her sleep.
Some days you take what victories you can.

The Trembling Cup

No matter how hard I try, I can't remember
who knocked on the door
and why I answered

and drank what was offered,
only that I must have,
because it's still seeping through my veins

decades later. Did someone force apart my lips
or did I take the cup willingly?
How could a day I'm not sure happened

change my life? Maybe if I remembered
the exact moment my life turned wrong,
if I had a date and time,

I could go back and forgive my hands
for taking the cup
and my throat for swallowing its poison.

Adam
Albrecht Dürer—1507

When the young cop tells me to hold out my arms,
I'm disappointed the cuffs aren't metal.
It's hard to feel noble if you're shackled
in plastic. Then another cop
who happens to look like my sixth-grade teacher
presses on my shoulders and sits me down
on the school bus as if we were all going on a fieldtrip
instead of to jail. I thought I'd get chained
to a Marxist. Instead it's a powdery woman
about as radical as Whistler's mother.
Everyone is singing *If you're happy and you know it,*
clap your hands, as if the truest forms of protest were irony
and whimsy. I've been busted
with a bus full of Dadaists instead of a paddy wagon
of Pete Seegers steeped in so much sorrow
people would put aside their weed killer
and turn off their gas grills and follow us
the way the apostles did Jesus
or at least the hippies did Abbie Hoffman,
as if it were possible, even in Bucks County, Pennsylvania
for people to see the light.
The light that matters right now
is the one that seems to have decided
not to change at the intersection of Rt. 611
and Burnt Hollow Road. I turn to the window
of another yellow bus, this one carrying kids home
from high school, and the boy gazing back
reminds me so much of Dürer's Adam before the Fall
I touch two fingers to my lips

and press them to the window as his bus pulls away.
The glass takes my fingerprints:
a little maze of loops
and whorls yet another hand has left behind
before going on to other quixotic pursuits.

Untitled (Black on Gray)
Mark Rothko—1969-70

1

What I see is the world before God got cold feet and said,
Let there be light. A sky that resists sharing the universe with
the sun—or any star. *The palpable obscure?* Genesis before
it was turned into a soap opera? I see a sky that's profoundly
uninterested in what we might say about it and that doesn't
want anything to spoil its bad mood. A dark so dark it is
nothing but supremely itself.

2

Let's visit the Guggenheim, my wife suggests. We walk the
fifteen blocks from the train station because we don't know
how much to tip a cab driver and still have enough left for
souvenirs for the kids. It's becoming clear to me I'll never
be more than meteorite debris in the galaxy, but my wife
tells me to stop talking and enjoy the pictures. We stand the
requisite eighteen inches away from Rothko, but neither
of us says what we're thinking. I keep being pulled closer
till I fear I'll plunge into that fabulously expensive darkness
and the guards will come running. I shove my hands in my
pockets. It won't be the first time they've got me in trouble.
Go ahead, I hear each Rothko whisper. *Your life will never
be the same.* When I finally think to look at my wife, she's
crying and won't say why. *Let's go,* I say because sometimes
that's the only thing to do: pick up your coats and step into
the light you know will solve nothing.

3

Years later, I find *Untitled (Black on Gray).* Though it's been
shrunk to five by eight inches, it's colossal. Half of the
darkness belongs to sky, the other half to ocean and just as

vast and committed to staying as it is. Water uncontaminated by living organisms. Water that reflects nothing and upon which you detect God's thumbprint. The waters of Day Three with nothing on the horizon except a gray streak too smeared to illuminate anything. A sea not expecting to be crossed, even by light. A sea asking and hoping for nothing.

Roll Call

The kid who never takes off his tasseled cap,
even when it's eighty degrees outside.
The girl who goes nowhere without Proust,
but confesses she'll read halfway through a chapter
in *Remembrances of Things Past*
before she realizes she's read it before.
Her friend suspended in high school
for setting her English classroom and *Paradise Lost* ablaze,
The boy who could've made a living
in the sixteenth century playing Ophelia or Juliet.
The kid who covers notebooks with photos
of his buddies racing each other into the surf.
That's me and my cousin Jared and my best friend Matt,
the summer Matt's father died.
The girl who sits sideways every class
because she's got more important things to do
than look at her teacher—what good ever came of that?
The boy next to her with eyes so cobalt
it makes her own eyes seem imitation blue.
The heavy-set girl with facial hair,
who all semester has made it painfully clear
I'm not the professor she hoped for:
one who'd wax so eloquently about poetry
life would seem worth living.
The skinny girl with glasses too big for her face,
who asks, *May I write my research paper on the diabolic?*
I can get twenty-five pages out of demons.
The young man who runs sentences together
as if punctuation had no business interrupting him.
The kid next to him, who on principle never

laughs at anything his teacher says
but, like a knife sheathed, glares at me
as if his eyes have the power to cut me open.
All present and accounted for.

What to Do the Day a Camera Is Shoved Up Your Ass

First splash water on your face:
remind it that it too must wake up.

The cats don't care about your soon-to-be invaded
rear end. They're clear on their priorities:

Feed them. Then pry your grandson out of bed,
his arms thrown over his pillow

as if he's in a shipwreck he's not sure he's going to survive.
Persuade him to eat his toast,

that cosmic insult you've set before him.
After he's off to school, vacuum the rug of toast crumbs;

abandon the house in reasonably good shape
so when your wife comes home from her business trip

she won't find the mess she expects.
At school let yourself get excited again

about "Ozymandias." Choke back a few tears
when you read a poem by a girl surprised—

almost by accident—by how she really feels.
Afterwards visit a young man in jail

you've been helping to write a letter
to his father who used to tie him to a chair

and scream to him about his mother.
Finally you can't put it off any longer:

head for the doctor's
down a highway lined by so many trees

it's like running a gauntlet.
A woman at the desk smiles

as if sincerely glad you didn't cancel
and another woman shows you to a room

where on the walls there's nothing to look at
except others humans' glossy insides,

and then an attendant, your son's age, wedges a camera
between your buttocks, saying, *It's okay, it's okay!*

while your rectum severely disagrees,
and then the doctor starts taking bites out of your prostate

like he's punching staples in
for the fun of it—the way you used to, as a kid,

not trying to hold anything together
just wanting to see how much paper could take.

It doesn't hurt, does it?
the doctor asks again and again.

No, you say as you shudder with each click of the gun,
Are you going to stop soon?

For a week after, you have to sit down
to pee, your body needing all the assistance it can get.

Otherwise, things go on as usual:
the cats must still be fed,

your grandson cajoled out of bed,
fragments must still be ferreted out of sentences.

The only difference for now—it'll take five business days
for the biopsy report—is that you're pissing blood.

How odd that sounds! *You're pissing blood.*
Not everyone in America can say that.

Reading about Beauty in the Hospital

While my wife is recovering from the operation
we hope tracked down the cancer,
I can't stop sneaking looks at her roommate,
the one with a voice that sounds like dishes falling;
hair so black you'd expect to see stars in it;
and two children who poke and chase each other
from one side of the bed to the other
fractious as squirrels.
While my wife slips in and out of sleep
I read *The Testament of Beauty*
and try not to doze over this book
my father nagged me to open
while he was still alive.
As the woman lifts herself from bed
to wheelchair, I try not to
turn to the place where her thighs should be.
Instead I make myself focus
on her cherubic son and winsome daughter
too busy plotting against each other
to care their mother has no legs.

Maybe It's Not Scruples That Save Us

The girl shooting hoops at the town park?
The boy at his remote controls
making his speedboat go in circles so fast
it almost leaps out of the water?
You must be in good shape
to follow a child for blocks and blocks
till your legs question the effort
especially if the kid turns out to have bad breath
and acne. Plus, you must immediately forget the lad
has another life besides the one you're about to write
a backstory for. It's no small task
to deconstruct a boy from the messy
exigencies of his daily life till he's text,
pure and ephemeral, for your fingers to improvise on.
I could no more coax a child out of his clothes
than I could persuade a stranger to buy a car
or go into a voting booth and pick me
out of all the other candidates.
Seducing a child demands a sword-swallower's impeccable
timing, a theater critic's supreme
confidence, the patience of a CIA agent
or a birdwatcher, the steady nerve of an air traffic controller
talking down a Piper Cub piloted by a kid
whose father's just had a heart attack.
You can't let the boy sense any doubt in your voice.
At fifteen I let a man interrogate my body
in a public rest room. He must've seen how tired I was
after football. I wasn't submitting to sex
but being tutored in a trade
I later decided against. Not just on moral grounds.
It's much too much work.

Having devoted years to warning my sons away
from speeding cars, poisonous berries, ledges,
shielding them from fractions, boredom, heroin, and other bullies,
I can't imagine having enough energy
left over to lure someone else's antsy kids into a car
no matter how pretty they might be.
Maybe it's not scruples that save us
but exhaustion. I can't be the only one tempted
at the curve of a mountain road to spin
the steering wheel, turn guardrails irrelevant,
carry another person with me to eternity—
you, boy with your head so far in a book
you could be a bee immersed in pollen;
you, girl wiping smudges off your bike's handlebars
as it if it's important
to get at least one place clean in the world.

One More Rosewood Box of Ashes

1

Try as I do, I can't wash the stink out of the fur
of my Siamese. That's the trouble with urine
and dried feces. Even if you get rid of the smell
you smell it all day.
Today Old Yang visits the hair salon
Sadie has set up
in our living room. He proves as good a customer
as any. He sits still
and even lets Sadie tug her comb through the mats
on his belly
before it's time for her to go to school.
Goodbye, Old Mr. Yang,
Sadie fully expects to see him tomorrow
because she saw him yesterday.
For twenty years this cat has put up with my complaints
against the world. He's seen me naked.
He's slept with my wife as often
as I have, these past two decades
and caused her much less trouble.
I pat him in the vet's waiting room,
I tell him it will be all right.
It won't be.

2

not dead
not dead
not dead
not dead
not dead
not dead

                              not dead
                                 d
                                 e
                                 a
                                 d
                                 !

3

It's tomorrow.
We are already talking of Yang in the past tense.

I am sorry.
What else do you say
to someone with whom you've shared a bed
and then one day decide to kill?
He was old. He had a good life.
He's not suffering anymore.
There was nothing else you could do.
There was.

4

You can't call out of work if your cat has died.
Don't expect a visit from the minister.
You won't get sympathy cards.
Your children ask when you're going to get another cat.
Your grandchildren talk nostalgically
about pets that followed them when they were babies.
You don't say much to your wife,
she doesn't say much to you.
That's the way with grief:
once you begin falling
you keep falling.

5

Dearest ones, when I'm feeble,
you won't have the option of putting me to sleep
though I'll probably smell
even worse than old Yang.
When I'm finished dying, go home
and burn all my hoarded treasures
as I did with Old Yang's,
the stuffed animals the grandkids threw away
and I shampooed after I dug them out of the trash,
all the beat-up sneakers I never could part with,
the rough drafts of poems I saved
in case one improbable day I was famous.
Make a fire high enough
to roast marshmallows.
Remember how I liked mine: charred
almost all the way through
so black you couldn't imagine eating anything
this crinkly and ruined.
In a day or two
buy a cat,
one that promises to live forever.

Happiness Anonymous

I can wade Grief –
Whole Pools of it –
I'm used to that –
But the least push of Joy

Jesse's only seventeen but he's already counting the hours
he has left to live. Every day he does the math
over again: all that time wasted taking out trash
or trying to comb a part into his hair
or persuading *x* to equal *y*. On a day this sunny
in a land noticeably free of pestilence and plague
you'd have to be ingenious to find anything to fret about
but Jesse succeeds.

As if the sun's one true purpose were to tempt him
to throw off the years of sobriety,
Stefan sits with his back to windows. At five
he had made the mistake of playing
too long and, when he got home, found his mother
in a corner, one hand clutching the other like a wounded bird.
He loosened her fist from around the broken glass.

Last week Sylvia's Tyler took his first wobbly steps
and tottered before her like a drunk
who suddenly grows aware he's got a left and a right side
and needs to persuade them to take turns
and share this tipsy planet. *Babysitting's so difficult.*
She can't stop imagining
all that's waiting to harm her grandson.

Why can't you be happy? Roger's wife complains.
She acts, he grouses, as if she'd just found him cheating.

His sons, on principle, refuse to forgive him too:
who wants a father who can't watch the news without crying?
Yes, kids are abducted into slavery in Sudan,
but, Roger's wife likes to remind him, this is Levittown, PA.
No soldiers are disemboweling anyone on Sycamore Drive today.

Regret, remorse, grief, foreboding, dread, and despair.
Yep, I'm in the right support group.
What more loyal comrades could one want?
"Hi, I'm Kip. It's been 4,092 days and 6 minutes
since I last took a swig
of joy, a snort of pleasure, a nip of delight."

"Welcome, Kip."

IV.

We read the news. Bread should turn to dust,
to fire; but we chew, we swallow.

Luray Gross

Saturn Devouring One of His Children
Francisco Goya y Lucientes—1823

You don't have to be a kid to be spooked by this father
tearing his son apart limb
by limb as if it were only natural for a parent
to get so sick of his children
he devours them. The more I gaze at Goya's painting,
the more it changes before my eyes.
At first Jupiter's father glares at us
as if we'd just flung open a door he'd bolted shut.
Then the rage on his face flickers
into bafflement as if maybe it's not too late
to turn back from the crime
to which he's committed. Then he's a dog
cornered and not about to give up
what he's gnawing. Surely I am not the only father
terrified of the harm he could inflict
on his children, though it's unlikely
I'm going to make a late-night snack of my son
or rip my daughter's arm off
and feed on it. Yet what parent hasn't done enough
awful things to suspect he or she could do more,
to want to avoid mirrors, yet
still keep turning away and back
to this painting, the mind
revealed in all its voraciousness.

Pain Management

No. Stop it, right now! My father pushes away my hand,
with each button I undo. It even hurts him
to be naked. I loosen his drawstring,
peel his soiled undergarment away, gather him up.
No, a thousand times no! I can't stand it.
my father begs as I slip one arm under his shoulders

and the other under his knees,
the way a husband carries a bride over the threshold.
My dad might be dying, but at least he knows
to hold on to my neck.
For months I've been afraid this will be the evening
my father's body tires of the hard work

required to keep breathing. *You'll feel better*
if we just get your scalp clean,
I whisper. Why do I believe if I hush, he will?
It never worked with my two-year-old.
Put me down. Now! On the stool where I settle him
my dad fidgets as my son used to

in his time-out chair. *How could you do this to me?*
my father howls not just at me
and my mother huddled in the hallway
and his granddaughters reading books
they've brought, this visit, to hide behind
but at the whole world—

NO! NO! Even before I slip the shower hose
off its sprocket and spray water
as lightly as I can over his shimmering neck,
his belly, and shrunken buttocks,

make the hot and cold come to a truce
before they attack my father's spindly legs

A thousand times no! he bellows.
After I've toweled him dry,
my mother holds his pajama top away from his chest
so he'll not be irritated by our fingers'
familiar quarrels with his buttons.
No, as he's lifted onto the hollows

in the bed his body counts on returning to,
where I ease first one, then another thin pillow
under his head. *No,* he mutters,
falling asleep before his eyes do.
No, no, no, say the breaths
my father's body takes without intending to.

I've heard that prayer before.
It doesn't really mean *no.* It doesn't really mean *yes.*
No, I tell my mother, let him rest.
No, I tell my daughters. *Go back to your books.*
No, I promise there's no need to be scared.
Yes, I'll leave the light on.

The Butter Knife

My mother's got a knife and it doesn't matter
                    that she's ninety-five
and it's only sharp enough to cut butter,
                    she's going to
plunge it into the throat of the deaf woman
                    to her right,
she's going to use it to murder
                    the blind woman to her left
who won't stop moaning, in other words
                    being so obviously old.
That's one of the benefits of having dementia:
                    you don't have to listen
to reason or remember past kindnesses,
                    the aides who sang to you
as they changed your diapers
                    or tucked you into bed.
The blade is a kite escaped from its line.
                    It's a bird trapped
in a room of windows. It slices the air
                    into hundreds of pieces.
This morning I happen to show up
                    in time
to grab the knife in mid-wield
                    before my mother
can drive it into a nurse's heart. It doesn't
                    even break the skin
though I feel the blade
                    in my hand
hours afterwards, the punishment
                    it intended, its refusal
to compromise, its principled rage.

Ode to the Spoon

That it's no bigger than a thumbprint
and invites the thumb to rub its belly.

That it has a belly
taking only a second to fill.

That it was forged in a fire
no human could hope to survive,

so my mother might enjoy her tapioca,
which tastes better if it rides to the tongue on silver—

I discovered later was silver plate.
That my mother wanted me to believe

I was eating from something not so different
from what the Queen lifted to her lips

and what I lift now to my mother's lips.
She's so old she's outgrown forks and knives.

That a Thanksgiving dinner can be served
on a single spoon: pureed turkey,

pureed asparagus, pureed pumpkin pie.
That even the word *spoon* is easy on the mouth.

That it asks so little of the lips—just opening.
That my mother must be reminded to swallow.

That it doesn't discriminate, bitter or sweet.
That it bears good news to her mouth.

What Happens When You Die?

What if the minister is right and we live forever
as pure thought? Imagine the freedom
to hold a grudge for a century

or devote a millennium to a single worry,
to have infinity to mope. Do the evil, once deceased,
put what they've committed out of mind,

Hitler or General Custer or Miss Mansure
who made my son stand in a pool of his own urine
till the bell rang and the class tired of laughing at him?

And what about my cat hit by the neighbor's car?
Does he have to relive in his mind the moment of impact?
And my neighbor, will he feel guilty

till the ice caps melt and there are no such things
as cats? Maybe in a million years
I'll forget the boner I got in the seventh grade boys' shower

or the party where I threw up on the girl I was trying to impress
or the words I shouted at my daughter that made her cry.
With a million more, maybe I'll get over the slap

I gave my brother two days before he neglected to brake
and entered a coma we thought he'd never
escape, though he was back in school, a month later.

Live forever? I have trouble
just getting though a day.
How can I possibly fill up all that time?

Open the Door

1

Oh Herb, you used to say, *come quick.*
There'd be a mole chewing on whatever moles feast on
or a spider busy reconstructing its universe
in a corner of your porch
and even though Herb was inventing a program
he was sure would expand all human thought
he'd get up from the computer
and go to the window
because saving the world would have to wait
for a centipede making its way efficiently over the sill
or a nuthatch selecting not *this* tiny twig
but *that* one—the fate of its nest depending
on it picking the right piece of packing string,
the perfect strand of dog hair.

2

Those were years we had the luxury
of devoting afternoons to remembering
pencil boxes and slide rules,
mechanical pencils, old grammar school teachers.
Your daughter hadn't died yet,
my father hadn't got around to trying to kill himself,
and so, once a week,
we'd carry Earl Grey up three flights
to my attic office with a tray of walnuts, hard cheese,
grapes—no one ought to talk poetry
on an empty stomach!—and sip
the steam off our cups
because part of the pleasure of tea lies in the little scolding
it gives the tongue,

and you'd act as if my new poem wasn't confessing
the exact same thing
my last poem did. You loved words that much
you didn't mind if they repeated themselves.

3

Once there was a woman who thought snow was hers
to keep and she wouldn't be dissuaded
not even by her therapist who warned
she'd never get over her daughter's death
till she stopped being distracted by the drifts
against her house, their *frolic architecture.*

She'd stand at the windows
as if she owed each snowflake her full attention:
some throwing themselves against the windows;
some curtseying as if being presented at a ball;
some floating like ships headed off
somewhere no one can follow;
some collapsing as if it's finally too exhausting
being one of a kind.

4

I didn't realize how many poems you'd written
about snow till I came upon a flurry
in your apron pockets, a blizzard
in a cooking pot, a whole nest of haikus
in your sewing basket
as I helped to empty your house of its 2,850 tin cans
washed and sorted by size,
its 422 baskets, its 512 bolts of fabric, its 9,233 books—
some falling apart as soon as I opened them,
some housing bugs I didn't recognize,
some smelling so bad even I couldn't read past the first page,

ursi everywhere:
a grizzly in a waistcoat, a marsupial in a bow tie,
neon green and psychedelic pink pooh bears
on top of heating ducts,
behind cereal boxes, on windowsills,
an almost life-size Himalayan in the spare bathtub
that'd stopped working years ago,
so many so moldy my grandkids and I filled our sled
and dragged polar bears and pandas into the woods.
Let the rain decide what to do with them
and their bifocals and ribbons.
Let the worms and the foraging birds consult
with those final arbiters, air
and earth, able as earth and air are
to put up with all our bad smells, our good intentions.

5

You wouldn't find it crazy
that I still leave forsythia at your doorstep,
stones I've picked up, knowing
your thumb would appreciate their smoothness,
that even now I show up at the front door
of the house from which your friends and I rescued
D's scrapbooks of horses,
Wendy's and Elf's wheelchairs,
their hospital johnnies, their tic-tac-toe games,
charcoal sketches you drew of them,
every poem Herb jotted on a grocery bag,
his old Boy Scout uniforms,
his general semantics textbooks, floppy discs
that'd survived their computers,
bird guides, auto repair manuals, murder mysteries,
books devoted to copper piping and knots,
waves and light,

and outside by the garage even a few crates of poetry
trying to survive the snow and rain.
It's not that I'm in the neighborhood
but still I check your mailbox,
pick up the branches the last storm blew down,
and knock and knock
as if maybe time made a terrible mistake.
Years ago when your mother died—
too many miles away for you to rescue her—
I'd pounded and pounded at this same door.
I'd wanted to be the one to comfort you—
that old greed in me
to be the one friend you could not live without.
So I went to the windows and called your name,
tapped on the glass
till my fingers got tired of their polite inquiry
and started banging, almost
daring the panes to break. I hammered at the door
as if it were responsible for your deafness.
I knew you were inside
sleeping. As if the only way to bear your pain
was for you to close your eyes and keep them closed.

6

I'd moved you into this house, one Halloween night,
you and I and Herb on the U-Haul ramp,
walking a refrigerator down
full of texts you'd marked up
with exclamation points—no greater pleasure
than reading a book for the second time
or the third, you'd said. In the freezer
Betsy Sholl, Joan Aleshire, Natashe Saje,
Bill Wunder, Lucille Clifton, Lorraine Henrie Lins,
Luray Gross, Deda Kavanagh, George Drew,

Wendy Fulton Steginsky, Pat Goodrich,
Bernadette McBride, Marie Kane,
Elizabeth Raby, Hayden Saunier, Sandy Becker,
Lynn Levin, Diana Weiss, Cornelius Eady,
Camille Norvaisas—as if you were testing
how many poets you could pack
into a fridge. And now
here I am shouting at your door again
so loud someone might think I'm a madman
and you the only one who could save me.
My knuckles are bleeding but still I rap
and rap as if desperation ever convinced a door
to open, as if I couldn't be in this much pain
and it not count for something.
Damn it, open the door, Pamela.
Open the door.

My True Vocation

Did you see that? I ask Tyler.
Did you hear that, Josie? It's my job as grandfather
to add a little adventure to their day,
a secret panel, a passageway even the dead don't know,
a banshee or two to hide from,
an opportunity to be braver than we dared
believe we could, holding our breath
in the storage closet of a building so old
it doesn't take much imagination
to think it haunted. Maybe this time I've gone too far.
A week later Tyler's still looking for mummies
in the library, at school, at the doctor's office.
Josie demands to know if her teacher's a poltergeist
in disguise, and so I get a good scolding.
I don't remind my son and his wife
I've been on this earth long enough
to find it disappointing
without a little astral projection, shadows lurking
to relieve the intolerable equanimity
of light. If I invent occasional dangers
for my grandkids, maybe they'll get so busy
outsmarting vampires and goblins
real terrors won't be able to harass them.
At my age, I'm not that many years away
from learning whether I'll get to be disembodied
spirit, a different retirement
than what I expect my wife had in mind for me,
but a better promotion than I'll ever win
at my real job, working conditions
in many ways superior to what my body provides.
Maybe I've been preparing for this employment

all my life: to follow my grandchildren's every move
from the grave as only an apparition can, intimate as air
but unable to interfere, wishing all well
and wishing so hard,
perhaps they'll feel that wish in a curtain's
fluttering, the flickering of a light.

The Trainset

For JHB 1977–2012

After a day of being paid to compromise
it must've been a relief to come home to trains
that went about their business as single-minded
as bees—rivers you sent running
into the lake waiting patiently below.
You even took off the doors everywhere upstairs
so the tracks could run from room
to room, left a second-story window partially open
so the metropolis you'd created
got to experience the same weather you did.
You'd put in too many hours to call this a hobby,
too much money to profit from it,
too much frustration with recalcitrant springs
and uncooperative gears for it to be merely
escape. Cliffs and glens, silver mines, and waterwheels
and tunnels so dark and long
we were relieved to see your engines finally reappear
at the other end. The few of us lucky enough
to be invited up to the world you'd created
were always surprised by the small
yet important alterations you made to your layout:
a fishing hole and a child baiting his hook,
or a wolf on the scrub pine ledge
staring at a passing train as if they were equals.
A pickup truck idled at the junction
of Jerusalem Road and Rosethorn Lane
in the village whose streets you'd named
so its tiny inhabitants could find their way to the pharmacy
or hardware store you'd built for them.
From their circus train giraffes and tigers gazed down

on all the humans forced to wait upon their progress
at the crossings you'd crafted
just for the pleasure of stopping traffic
so your Silver Streaks and Crescent Moons could run on schedule
long after most sensible people would've gone to bed,
an entire city gone black
till it was completely up to the stars
to see that there was light.
Where else could you get to live in a world
of your own making? If we happened to believe in God,
we could ask Him what that's like
and if one doesn't believe in God,
well, that's yet another reason to have a trainset.

She's Here Now!

Not till he was dead did my father quit worrying
about the size of his penis. *Brain-damaged*,
the doctors had said to explain why he wouldn't stop bragging

about his whores, even after he grew so thin
there was barely any body left to take in my arms.
It felt like bathing a phantom, my mother and I wondering

if any moment he might dematerialize.
And now my mother is an apparition too
though she haunted my father long before he hit that tree.

Even in his mistress's arms, my dad heard my mother
fluttering like a ghost through his illicit rooms.
She's here now! He made me look

under the hospital bed, in the closet, nowhere safe
from her claim on him. While I wait for the undertaker
in my mother's hospice room I'd filled

with enough of her things it'd seem to belong to her:
her oil paints, her berets, her walking sticks,
a wind-up nun, beach heather, a jar of sea-glass,

a lighthouse that actually blinked
in case ships sailing though the Phoebe Berks Personal Care Unit
needed some warning.

My mother's son, I've got to keep my hands busy now,
even if it means working around her corpse,
sorting what I can bear to keep, what I can't

bear to throw away till I find myself bumping
against her bed and whispering *sorry*—
no one, it seems, ever done apologizing to his parents.

Maybe even ghosts ought to be free to indulge
in a little sentimentality. There's a whole world
for my mother and father to haunt now,

and I won't be able to think a single thought
without them pushing their way back
into my mind. Apparently they intend to stay,

at least till I'm a phantom myself
spooking my own children.
Though I don't trust in God, I choose to believe something

transpires when an idea leaps from one neuron's
spidery branches to the spidery
branches of another. Maybe a wraith

haunts the synapses. Listen, children. That'll be me
making my leap of faith
across the great divide between axon

and dendrite, flitting through what you've come
to call thought, your father, most faithful
of ghosts, and just as troublesome as I am now.

The Account Books of J. H. Bursk Wholesale Grocers

As a young child, I stared in fascination as my father cut his nails; even his cuticles held clues. Showering with him after tennis, I stole glances in case his penis might unfold a secret no other part of him could. And when he got so old I had to change his diapers, my fingertips found themselves puzzling over his skin's smoothness.

Insurance bills, lecture notes, cancelled stock certificates, a college literary magazine. I'm still searching my father's files for proof of what he hid from me. Does this happen with everyone who goes through a parent's papers: you own a book for years and, one day, out falls a letter you never noticed before?

It's easy to miss the Latin in these ledgers, buried as it is behind two years of string beans. It took me a week to decipher one passage. I wasn't my father's son when it came to ablative absolutes. What had transpired in my parents' marriage to prompt my father to translate the letters of star-crossed Heloise and Abelard? Was he keeping up his Latin? If so, why not Martial or Marcus Aurelius? Why, instead of going home at night, did my father linger at his gradually discounted and depleted warehouse with a castrated monk?

Considering that one sentence in the middle of the ledger runs over 200 words long and takes more turns than Theseus in the Minotaur's maze, it's unlikely my mother read my father's translations. Maybe she wanted nothing to do with legumes or Latin. With no PhD and three boys to care for, she'd little time for the woes of Heloise and Abelard.

The world might be at war, his alcoholic father's business going bankrupt, his mother's house emptying of heirlooms, his one son refusing to nurse, another to sleep alone, but my father had this delight: the unobstructed beauty of contrapuntal clauses, nothing undeclined, nothing left unconjugated, everything accounted for. At least he could keep something from collapsing, even if only a periodic sentence or two.

What am I to do with these mildewed books, this crumbling Latin? Like so much sons discover as they seek to make sense of their fathers, these ledgers only complicate. Are we in the red or black? No matter how long we pore over our parents' books, do they ever balance? Father and sons; what a long and difficult collaboration and even longer and more difficult translation. One I hereby bequeath to my sons.

More Reasons You're Thinking of Killing Yourself

Because it's embarrassing how many poems you've written
about killing yourself.

Because you discovered the suicide note
your father wrote to your mother.

Because the note said, *I'm sorry, dearest,*
our sons didn't turn out as we hoped.

Because your oldest friend just died
after you'd been angry with her the whole year

for only taking half of every pill prescribed her.
Because she wouldn't let you in her house

of newspapers piled to the ceiling.
Because she'd been the only person you trusted

with your suicide notes disguised as poems,
only she didn't find you morally irresponsible

for wanting to kill yourself.
Because your father didn't die from that bottle of pills,

but drifted off to sleep
after you spent a year changing his diapers

sprinkling talcum powder on his buttocks
and sending him into his dreams smelling like a baby.

And you're still hanging onto self-pity
because it's something you've always been good at:

far easier than grieving,
you'd rather do anything than grieve.

Abraham and Isaac

This morning, Tyler's eager to play Abraham and Isaac
before kindergarten, so he needs a sharp knife,
a sheep, and a son. Maggie and Sadie
quarrel over whose turn it is to be the trembling boy,
and then Sadie prepares to be sacrificed
on the rock (the hassock we chase Peaches the cat off).
Maggie's content with the wings
I keep handy. *Stop wriggling!* Tyler commands,
holding the dagger just over Sadie's bare belly,
but his taped-on beard muffles the words
and gets Sadie giggling till I must coax Tyler back
from the kitchen. As a toddler
he'd trip over his feet and get angry at the floor
for not breaking his fall, so he's perfect
as Father of the Israelites, his capacity to take affront
biblical. Though he demands a real knife,
he settles for a plastic flamingo. Even Abraham must
make do, especially with only a half hour
before the bus. Refusing to beg for mercy, even if the Bible
requires it, Sadie holds every part of her still
till Maggie pops out from behind the bush,
ram in hand (you guessed it: Peaches the cat)
and shrieks so loud it'd be hard to believe her an angel,
if it wasn't for her flapping wings.
Tyler pretends not to hear the messenger of the Lord
(no easy task, given Maggie's decibels).
I can see he's tempted to rewrite the Bible and slaughter Isaac,
so I step out of the audience, the Lord Almighty,
and in my deepest voice shout *Abraham,
Abraham!* and plop Peaches in the exact spot
Sadie's vacated. Not yet three, she's old enough

to know when her cousin's so caught up
he can't help himself. Like Kierkegaard before him,
Tyler finds *the teleological suspends the ethical,*
though he doesn't make his case precisely
with those words. Thank God it's time
to get ready for school, brushing our teeth,
as if we hadn't just been on Mt. Gerizim
with blood on our hands.
Just before Tyler gets on the bus,
he turns to me and whispers so the others can't hear,
I forgot to tell Sadie I love her.
This young man knows his Old Testament.

Why I Go In and Out of Jail

1

When I was boy visiting my hospitalized mother
I had to go through three locked gates.
Each had its own special sound
when it clicked shut. It's not that different here.
No door slams shut the same way.

2

If you've done Ecstasy,
I tease my students in jail,
what's the harm of a little metaphor?

3

Listen, Tiny, the safecracker interrupts class
one morning so dreary
we can feel the clouds getting ready
to punish us. *Put your ear to this sonnet.*
Hear the tumblers fall?

4

Today I ask everyone in our cramped classroom
to imagine what guardian angel they'd have
if they weren't too old or cynical
to have a guardian angel.
Give him or her a name,
I tell them. Some afternoons my class will do anything
to humor me: *Israfel, Jophiel, Zabaniyah, Maalik,*
Uzziel, Raphael, Gabriel, Phosphorus,
and, of course, *Lucifer.*

5

If someone had opened my bedroom door
when I was eleven
he or she might've heard me speaking a language so foreign
it couldn't be attached to a country
already on the map. I wasn't talking to myself.
The visitor might've seen just one person
in the room—me—
but, be assured, there were two.

6

You work in jail? my new neighbors ask
in the same voice my fifth-grade classmates used
when I admitted to them I spent my afternoons
with an imaginary friend.
No one invents an imaginary friend
because he's useful, but because he's not.
He'll cause all kinds of problems.

7

The man who talks to the voices in the radiators,
the man who hid from the cops in a dumpster,
the man who exposes himself in libraries,
the man who beat up his mother.
If I expect my class to be honest,
maybe I need to be honest
too. Tell them about Alwyn,
my invisible companion till I was seventeen.

8

Seventeen? Who are you kidding?
Alwyn's still right here
next to you. He too puts a great deal of faith

in white space. In vision
and veto, in margins and metaphor.
He too listens for a door shutting.
He helps you write all your poems.
He's helping you finish this.

Ashes, Ashes, We All Fall Down

If I'm going to be ashes in a decade or so
why stay up past midnight staring at the television
as if it might have a change of heart
and show a third-party candidate winning office
or end the war, or cure my grandson's acne?
Maybe I should just enjoy the dog's howling next door.
All night it's been tugging at its chain
as if the links might finally get bored with being metal and snap.

If I'm going to be incinerated
in 3650 days or thereabouts, why am I sulking
because this morning of all mornings, my car tired of doing
the same thing it did the morning before
or because half my class chose not to show up for a lecture
that I, their professor, a year from retirement, hoped
would change their entire outlook
on comma splices? Once I'm ashes drifting on water,

what will it matter that I barfed on my senior prom date
or last week forgot my wife's sixty-first birthday
or today embarrassed my grandson in front of his friends?
How do any of us prepare for the future
when we're so busy making a mess
of the present? Perhaps this is time's truest revenge:
to make us aware of every minute
of its passing. And in approximately 5,256,000 minutes

from now—give or take a month or year or two—
my son is going to stand on a bridge
with his children and do what he'd never thought
he'd have to: let his quirky, annoying,
yet lovable father sift through his fingers.
I will be ashes so fine they won't even question the rocks
they fall on, the creek that sweeps them away.

The Perfect Knot

Last night I uncovered poems
hid so well it took me fifteen years to find them,
a ribbon tied around a packet of blue linen
as if whoever bound those sonnets
wanted whoever unwrapped them
to appreciate that some words ought to deserve more
than ordinary paper. It's my father's handwriting. His
rhymes grasp each other so earnestly
it's hard for me to keep reading.
I long . . . I yearn . . . I crave . . . I burn . . .
You sizzle . . . you spark.
Everything you touch turns bright.
Every day I am away from you is night.
You are my only light. My only dark.
Every noun is a tear, every verb a goodbye,
With each adjective I am preparing to die.
At first I can't tell if these are suicide notes
or love poems. To whom is my father speaking?
My mother? A mistress?
Someone so beautiful even the adverbs had to be beautiful
too, adjectives chosen
so every letter glides into the next,
every vowel nestles in a consonant's arms.
Why can't those we love be only
what we want them to be and perhaps only
what they wished to be?
There are secrets you whisper to your son
when you are dying, but there are other secrets
you wrap in dark purple ribbon
and hide—words too revealing to be published,
too important to throw away,

the kinds of poems old men write.
They know no one's going to read them
while they are alive
but they write them anyway. And save them.
See, I am writing one now.

Why I Don't Want My Grandchildren to Read My Poetry

1

Who wants a grandfather who writes poetry
about encouraging matches
to sink their talons into his skin,
all those burn marks on his arms, spent matches
in his desk drawers, their brief, doomed ignitions?
It's bad enough he hurts himself
but does he have to tell everyone?

2

Why must you be naked in so many poems?
my wife asks. It's not easy living with a man
who regularly goes up to his attic office
so he can be six again
and watch his mother dragged to an ambulance.
Or be fifteen and kissed by a stranger
in the back of a city bus.
Or be nineteen and dare the police again to catch him.

3

If I must write poems
they'd better not be about her.
That's my youngest granddaughter's final word
on the subject. I wish I could obey.

4

Grizzled addicts forever in recovery,
hard-working spin doctors,
storefront preachers, bodyguards,
flight attendants, nurse practitioners,
summer tutors, poor, put-upon familiars,

crotchety servants, old gossips,
words, it's you I've trusted
even though I've always known how bad you are
at keeping secrets.

5

If you are in a bookstore years after I've passed away
and by some fluke happen on a collection
by me, imagine the poems inside this volume
all say the same thing: *Thank you.*
You don't have to read me.
Put me on a high shelf. I'll be glad
just to have a place in your house.

Letter to a Great-great-grandson

Dear child-I-can-only-imagine,
there are advantages to being unborn:
no colic, no mushy peas to be tricked into eating,
no tug of war over potty training, or spelling tests,
no fractions to learn or girls to stammer in front of.
Your feet don't yet smell, nor your palms sweat.
No words stick in your throat.
You don't have to mope around the house
wondering if you'll ever get your driver's license
or manage the mechanics of making love.
Child, by the time you're born, I'll likely be long dead
but, if lucky, a ghost
who'd give anything for nocturnal emissions or a door to bang.
Will the seas have risen and taken back
what was theirs in the first place?
Will the price of gas be $30 a gallon?
Will there be pharmaceutical riots,
drugs doled out in church basements instead of soup?
Are the Cubs still trying to trade for a starting pitcher
to get them at last to the World Series?
Does spring still forget to arrive on time?
Or am I just another of those poets
who can't imagine being silenced,
egomaniac enough to insist on being heard
even after reduced to ashes? My verses
like the scribble of dew on the leaves this morning,
messages that'll vanish before anyone deciphers them?
Seed of a seed, if I can imagine you,
I can imagine a life to come.
This letter lets me do just that, each word
presupposing a future: the time in which it is written
implying a time afterwards in which it is read.

ACKNOWLEDGMENTS

Poems in this book have appeared in different versions in the following magazines: *Comstock Review, New Guard, Paterson Literary Review, Poetry Ink, The Sun, U.S. 1 Worksheets*—as well as in the Finishing Line chapbook, *The Boy with One Wing,* and in WordTech's *Unthrifty Loveliness.* Gratitude to Leah Maines of Finishing Line Press and Ken Waltzer of WordTech for helping so many voices to be heard.

The author wishes to acknowledge the support of his loving family and give thanks for the inspiration given him by the Bucks County poetry community; novelists Gregory Probst and Robert Stanton; professors Helen Lawton Wilson and Ethel Rackin; artists Bernadette Karpa and Steve Milner; editors Sy Safransky and Philip Fried; healers Rona Cohen, Anne Tax, and Peter Bridge.

This manuscript would not have been possible without the encouragement of Joan Aleshire, Lorraine Henrie Lins, and George Drew. Gratitude for guidance from April Ossmann, Baron Wormser, and Wyn Cooper and deepest thanks to all the CavanKerry community.

The cover is a print by Bernadette Karpa; the photograph of the author is by Jean Dolan.

CAVANKERRY'S MISSION

CavanKerry Press is committed to expanding the reach of poetry to a general readership by publishing poets whose works explore the emotional and psychological landscapes of everyday life.

OTHER BOOKS IN THE NOTABLE VOICES SERIES

Letters from Limbo, Jeanne Marie Beaumont
Tornadoesque, Donald Platt
Only So Far, Robert Cording
Unidentified Sighing Objects, Baron Wormser
How They Fell, Annie Boutelle
The Bar of the Flattened Heart, David Keller
Same Old Story, Dawn Potter
The Laundress Catches Her Breath, Paola Corso
American Rhapsody, Carole Stone
Impenitent Notes, Baron Wormser
Walking with Ruskin, Robert Cording
Divina Is Divina, Jack Wiler
How the Crimes Happened, Dawn Potter
Descent, John Haines
Southern Comfort, Nin Andrews
Losing Season, Jack Ridl
Without Wings, Laurie Lamon
An Apron Full of Beans: New and Selected Poems, Sam Cornish
The Poetry Life: Ten Stories, Baron Wormser
BEAR, Karen Chase
Fun Being Me, Jack Wiler
Common Life, Robert Cording
The Origins of Tragedy & Other Poems, Kenneth Rosen
Apparition Hill, Mary Ruefle
Against Consolation, Robert Cording

Printing this book on 30-percent PCW and FSC certified paper saved 2 trees, 1 million BTUs of energy, 127 pounds of CO_2, 67 pounds of solid waste, and 524 gallons of water.

The text for this book was typeset in Arno Pro, which was created by Robert Slimbach at Adobe. The name refers to the river that runs through Florence, Italy.